GARY AND NORMA SMALLEY

It Takes

Two

to

Tango

More Than 250 Secrets to Communication,
Romance and Intimacy in Marriage

Colorado Springs, Colorado

IT TAKES TWO TO TANGO
Copyright © 1997 by Gary and Norma Smalley. All rights reserved. International copyright secured.

Library of Congress Cataloging-in-Publication Data
Smalley, Gary.
    It takes two to tango / Gary and Norma Smalley.
        p. cm.
    ISBN 1-56179-460-0
    1. Marriage—United States.   2. Marriage—Religious aspects—Christianity.
I. Smalley, Norma.   II. Title.
HQ536.S635   1997
306.81—dc21   97-16424
                                                                 CIP

Published by Focus on the Family Publishing, Colorado Springs, CO 80995. Distributed in the U.S.A. and Canada by Word Books, Dallas, Texas.

Scripture quotations identified NIV are from the HOLY BIBLE, NEW INTERNATIONAL VERSION ®. Copyright © 1973, 1978, 1984 by the International Bible Society. Used by permission of Zondervan Publishing House. All rights reserved.

Photo on p. 32 by Cummings-Prentiss Studio.
Photos on pp. 103, 125, 147, 173 by Jim Lersh.

Editor: Larry K. Weeden
Front cover design: Candi Park D'Agnese
Front cover photo: Jim Lersh Photography

Printed in the United States of America

97 98 99 00 01/10 9 8 7 6 5 4 3 2 1

Contents

Introduction

*I*t's our pleasure to assure you, based on our own experience and that of hundreds of other couples we've observed and talked to, that your marriage can get better and better as the years go by. We've now been married more than 30 years, and we're happier together today than we've ever been. But as happy as we are, we expect the future to be even brighter!

You can have the same experience.

To help you do that, we've gathered in this book some of the best "nuggets" from Gary's teaching on what makes a marriage work. Many of them are gleaned from his best-selling video series "Hidden Keys to Loving Relationships."

But we also wanted in this book to give you my (Norma's) perspective on the aspects of marriage covered here. I'm a wife, the mother of three, and now a grandmother as well. (I also manage the day-to-day operations of our ministry, Today's Family.) And for all the years of our marriage, our relationship has been a partnership. We've learned and grown *together*. So together, we've written this overall introduction to the book and the introduction to each of its eight sections.

How could we do that effectively, we wondered, both of us writing, but each from a different perspective? We decided that the best way was to invite you to "listen in" to our dialogue as we discuss topics like honoring your wife, honoring your husband, learning to communicate, and building intimacy.

You'll find most of the "meat" about how to "tango" to a happy marriage in Gary's quotations. In our introductions, we'll tell some stories about how we've tried to live out those principles—and how we're still working at it after all these years!

Gary: For as long as I've been trying to help families, *honor* has been the central theme of my message. It's the single-most-important key to healthy, successful relationships.

That's why I'm thrilled that Norma, for the first time, is joining me in doing a book. I wouldn't be the man or husband I am today, with the ministry I have, and with the relationship we enjoy so much, if it weren't for her love and support over the years.

She has honored me by her excitement in agreeing to participate in this project.

Norma: As Gary's wife, I know he wants to honor me, and that has made such an impact on the quality of our relationship! He has grown enormously in this area, especially compared to the early years of our marriage.

That's not to say, of course, that he's now perfect and always honors me as he could. I'm not perfect either. But I know his intentions are good and his most basic desire is to honor me.

Gary: Let me show you how we still have to work at this crucial matter of honoring each other.

A short while ago, I—being a loving, sensitive husband whose whole ministry is based on the concept of honoring others—was talking to Norma on the phone, and in the course of our conversation I asked, "What do you need from me that I'm not giving you right now?"

She responded, "*You don't know how to honor me.*"

Naturally I laughed, assuming she was joking. I thought, *You can't be serious!* I said, "That's a good one! But what do you *really* need?"

And she said, "No, I'm not kidding. You don't know how to honor me."

Norma: I realized that at that moment, Gary and I were thinking of honor in different ways. He was thinking globally—big picture—and from that perspective he *does* do a good job of honoring me. He really works at it, and I enjoy and appreciate it very much.

But on this occasion, I was thinking of honor in a far more specific way. I was focusing on some things Gary does that bother me that I would put under the heading of "manners." I want him to have good manners, which I consider to be an important part of how a husband honors his wife and others.

For example, like most women, I take a lot of pride in my home. The way it looks affects the way I feel and also reflects on me as a homemaker. So if Gary wants to honor me, he should have the good manners to do his part to keep the house neat and picked up.

Well, Gary has a home office that's right off our kitchen and is very visible from there. And he keeps—I promise this is no exaggeration—20 pairs of shoes on the floor in that office! Every time I look over there and see those, I feel as if *I'm* not keeping up the house the way I should.

Just the other day, after working in the ministry office for 10 hours, I came home and found three pairs of his shoes sitting right in front of the TV in the family room!

Gary: Obviously, after all these years, we still need to work at this idea of honoring each other. And it *is* work!

In my mind, honor is a diamond. We started out with a rough, raw stone, and over the years I've made several major cuts and polishes, turning it into a beautiful gem. As far as I'm usually concerned, I'm doing a great job and it's ready to mount and display!

Norma, on the other hand, because she knows me better than anyone, realizes that there are still some rough surfaces, and she sees them all every day.

Norma: That just goes to show what we said earlier, that no matter how long we've been married, we still need to work at our relationship. We never want to take each other or our marriage for granted. In fact, that might be one of the best lessons you could take away from this book.

The quotations you'll find here are grouped into eight sections. You can read one quote a day as a sort of marital pick-me-up, or you can do a study on one of the eight topics at a time.

Whichever way you decide to use the material, beginning with our look at how a husband can honor his wife, we pray that it will help you and your spouse to turn your marriage into a lifelong tango of love!

Honoring
Your
Wife

Gary: Honoring your wife can mean many things to many people. As we saw in the introduction to this book, it often means *different* things to a husband and wife at a given point in time.

Norma: That brings up something I've seen over and over as I've asked literally thousands of men and women what *honor* means. Namely, when a husband does try to honor his wife, he usually does it from *his* point of view. He assumes he knows what she wants, when she may actually want something entirely different.

One of the best things a husband can do, then, is to ask his wife, "What does honor mean to you? How would you like for me to show you honor?" When she tells him what *she* wants, he can act out of knowledge instead of mistaken assumptions.

Gary: We were recently reminded that one of the key ways a man can honor his wife is by thinking about how the commitments he makes will affect her *before* he makes them.

I had come out with a new book of my own a few months earlier, and as often happens with a new book, the publisher asked me to go on a publicity tour to help generate some interest in it. Since I'm an outgoing person who loves to minister to people, I didn't have to be asked twice.

This was an extended, intensive tour that kept me on the road for three long, hard months. But I was having a great time! The people I was working with were terrific, and the audiences I spoke to responded warmly. As a result, a lot of good things were happening.

Things were going so well, in fact, that halfway through the tour, I was ready to sign up for a second tour that would start soon after the first one ended. *Surely Norma would want me to do this,* I figured.

It's a good thing I didn't lock myself into that commitment before I talked it over with Norma.

Norma: Gary was having so much fun—and helping so many people on the tour—that he didn't realize what was happening at home. Emotionally, I was hurting. I felt as if I had fallen from second place in his priorities, after God, to about fifth. I don't get jealous of all the attention Gary gets in his work, but I *am* bothered when he pushes me out of my rightful place.

In addition, his being gone so much and speaking in so many cities was putting incredible strain on our ministry staff. They, like me, were frustrated with the prospect of a second tour.

Gary: When Norma first told me she was opposed to my going on a second tour, I actually thought she was trying to block my future success. Can you imagine? Yet that's how blind I was to the impact the first tour was having.

But after she explained things, and after the members of our staff used word pictures to help me *feel* the burden they were carrying, I had no more desire to do the second tour. My fulfillment, after all, is in Christ, not in publicity tours.

Norma: Most of you husbands reading this won't be asked to go on book tours, because that's not the work you do. Yet you *are* asked all the time, like Gary, to make commitments that would have strong, direct impacts on your wives.

You might be recruited, for instance, to play on a recreational basketball team. "We'll play just one game a week," you're told. But what about practices and scrimmages and pickup games? That one-game-a-week commitment could actually consume three or four nights every week.

Does that mean you should never make such a commitment? Of course not. Who knows—maybe your wife will want to come to all the games and be your personal cheerleader. But the point is that you should think about the impact of the commitment on her—and better still ask her what she thinks of it—*before* you make it.

That's showing honor to your wife.

*H*usbands should realize that the words they speak to their wives have awesome power to build up or tear down emotionally. Affirming words are like light switches. To speak a word of affirmation at the right moment is like lighting up a whole roomful of possibilities.

*P*romise to tell your wife daily what you appreciate about her. Promise *yourself,* not her, because she might develop expectations and be hurt if you forget.

*W*hen a woman sees her husband's willingness to accept correction—a mark of someone who wants to gain wisdom—she's more willing to follow his leadership in the home because she values him more highly.

*L*ike a spacecraft, your marriage is subject to laws that determine its success or failure. If any of these laws are violated, you and your wife are destined to crash. However, if you recognize which law or principle you're violating and make the necessary adjustments, your marriage will stay on the right course.

*T*he major stumbling block for most husbands in developing a lasting love for their mate is failing to meet her needs *from her viewpoint.*

*D*on't be surprised if your wife doesn't understand your efforts to improve at first. It took at least two years before Norma would admit I was really changing. Now she knows I'm committed to spending the rest of my life developing our relationship and meeting her needs.

Wives need consistent proof of change over a period of time in at least three areas before they will believe their husband's commitment: careful listening without justification or argument, quickness to admit error, and patience with her doubts.

Your goal should be to become a genuine, loving, and tender husband who does not lecture. Lectures during stressful times only create more stress.

*I*f a husband can overlook the actual words his wife uses to express herself and instead actively pursue what she means, fewer arguments will take place.

*W*hen a wife is treated with tenderness and genuine love, she won't take advantage of the situation. The Scriptures teach that a husband is to *cherish* his wife (Ephesians 5:25), which basically means to protect her, especially in areas that cause her emotional or physical discomfort.

*I*f a man truly wants his wife to grow and the marriage to be strengthened, he should be the example of what he wants to see in her *before* saying *anything* to her.

A woman loves to build a lasting relationship with a man who cares about her enough to let her lean on him when she needs comfort. She needs a man who will understand her fears and limitations so that he can protect her.

*A*n incredible amount of hard feelings and conflict could be avoided if husbands would resolve not to make any decision affecting their wives and the rest of their families without first getting their wives' consent.

*L*et your wife teach you how you can best meet her needs during a crisis or when she's discouraged and losing energy.

When a man treats his wife carelessly, she's usually offended far deeper than he realizes. She begins to close him out, and if he continues to hurt her feelings, she will separate herself from him mentally, emotionally, and physically.

Genuine love is honor put into action regardless of the cost.

When a man learns to speak both the language of the head *and* the language of the heart, it can make tremendous positive changes in his own life and in the lives of his wife and children.

A woman misses very little about her environment, which is probably the basis for that mysterious gift some have called *intuition*—and another reason a man should honor and value his wife.

*V*aluing his wife's differences, and even taking the time to be a student of her needs, does *not* diminish the husband's leadership or responsibility in the family.

*B*ecause a woman's sense of value is so closely tied to the relationships around her, she's often gifted in helping her husband be more sensitive to what's really important beyond the immediate goal.

*W*hen she's expressing frustration, a woman doesn't need her husband's mouth, but his shoulder and arms.

*H*onoring your wife means protecting her like an offensive lineman forming a wall of protection in front of his quarterback. In football, there are rules to protect the quarterback from injury. Honor is the biblical principle God designed to protect each mate from being unnecessarily injured.

*W*hen you honor your wife, she will sense that nothing and no one in the world is more important to you. She won't have to wonder if she's number one—she'll know.

*Y*our wife has "fences" that protect her privacy or need for emotional space. When you respect these boundaries, it shows that you honor her requests.

*I*f you want to be considered great by your wife, start by learning to become a servant. Any time you promote her program or agenda over yours—without grumbling or complaining—you are sacrificially loving her.

*R*ecognize your wife's uniqueness. Because men and women are created differently, we need each other in order to grow toward maturity and balance. A woman may have more intuitive relational skills, but one of the strengths of a man is that he can decide to draw on those skills by asking probing questions like these: On a scale of 1 to 10, 1 being the worst and 10 the best, where do we want our relationship to be? Where is it, in general, today? What could we do in the next several days or weeks to bring our relationship closer to where we want it to be?

One simple way to honor your wife is by regularly showing that you appreciate her. Specific words of praise always score major points. Flattery is insincere or excessive praise. It's rooted in motives of self-interest; it implies you want something from her. True praise, on the other hand, focuses more on character qualities and is not self-serving.

A man needs to recognize the tremendous worth of his wife. Women have two incredibly important capacities because of the special way they're created. First, they have an intuitive desire to build meaningful relationships with those in their lives. Not only that, but they also have the capacity to recognize a healthy and intimate relationship. In a practical way, this means that a woman carries inside her a built-in marriage manual!

*I*f a woman has had a poor relationship with her father, she may have a hard time relating to her husband. The husband needs to realize he didn't cause this problem or some of the other things with which his wife struggles. However, he *is* responsible for his wife, and it's his job to find out what she needs for health and well-being.

*J*esus knew when His men were tired and needed to get away for some rest. One application for the husband is to be sensitive to when his wife needs a break from household responsibilities. He could offer to take care of the children for an evening so she can go shopping or do whatever else she desires.

Women want to be connected to their husbands, but men are naturally more comfortable keeping their distance. For the relationship to thrive, husbands need to learn the skills of connecting by meaningful conversation and by listening to the feelings and needs of their wives.

Men, when is the last time you looked your wife in the eyes and said, "I appreciate so much your emphasis on relationships and all you do to build ours up. The things you do to make our house into a home and the time you give to the kids—you're terrific"?

*W*omen will remember not only when they were offended, but also what the offender was wearing when the offense occurred. By following five steps after each offense, however—gentleness, understanding, confession, touching, and asking for forgiveness—a husband can begin to tear down the barriers that have sprung up to block the relationship.

*S*ome husbands and wives have built a high wall between them over the years. Each brick is an unconfessed and unforgiven act that closed the partner's spirit a little more. Just as it took time to build the wall, it will also take time to tear it down. If a husband will take the initiative to go back and deal with as many offenses as he and his wife remember, they will find tremendous healing.

*D*ifferences attract. But they can start to repel *after* the wedding. Husbands should value the differences as a gift that offers tremendous balance.

Honoring Your Husband

Gary: I have to acknowledge that women tend to be better at honoring their mates than men do. Nonetheless, there are things wives can learn, too, that will help them to show honor to the most important person in their lives.

Norma: One of the key ways a wife can honor her husband is to share in his interests—to get excited, at least to some extent, about the things that excite him.

For example, one time years ago, Gary and I both listed what would be a dream vacation trip for us, then exchanged lists. So I've known all this time (more than a decade) what he would really like to do in this area—a sailing and fishing trip where he can catch his dinner and have it cooked right up fresh. Because it wasn't something that appealed to me, however, I never showed any enthusiasm for it, and Gary has never taken that particular trip.

But this year, as I'm writing this, Gary is finally going to make that dream trip, and I'm going with him.

Gary: It means a lot to me that Norma wants to see that dream of mine come true *and* is willing to join me. She even organized it for me. I really do feel honored by that decision.

Another way she honors me is that she has learned to validate the fact that I have an off-the-wall kind of personality, and she's learning not to criticize or try to change who I am. I seem to come up with a new idea for something or other several times a day, for instance. In the past, as soon as I threw out one of these ideas, she would start shooting it down, pointing out what was wrong with it and all the reasons why it couldn't possibly work.

I felt as if my ideas were the clay pigeons at a skeet shoot, and she was the expert marksman!

Now, however, she listens and lets me have the fun of stating my ideas without immediately jumping in and blowing them out of the sky.

Norma: For the first 25 years of our marriage, I didn't realize that Gary thinks out loud—talking about an idea is the way he processes things. I thought that rather than just brainstorming, he was fully intending to do whatever he talked about, and it was up to me to figure out how to make it happen.

Once I finally understood his personality and the way he handles ideas, I also realized I didn't have to worry every time he came up with a new one. He wasn't really going to overturn our lives completely every couple of hours!

Part of how I've been able to honor Gary, then, was in learning enough about him to understand (better, at least) how he thinks. And that, in turn, made it possible for me to honor him by hearing out his ideas completely before offering any comments.

We're both a lot more fulfilled as a result.

*A*void being "hypersensitive" to every frown or smile from your husband. At all costs, put away anger if your husband doesn't follow through on developing the type of relationship you desire. Focus on what you have, not on what you don't have.

*A*s a wife, you and your marriage will experience less stress if you understand that men tend to be challenge-oriented and often lose interest once they've "conquered" or met the challenge. That's why they can be so romantic before marriage and afterward show little interest in romance.

*A*s a wife, you need to understand these differences between men and women: By nature, a woman tends to relate to others on a more personal level, while a man tends to be more challenge-and-conquer oriented. . . . A woman finds much of her identity through her relationships, while a man usually finds his identity through his accomplishments. . . . A woman is usually much more in touch with her emotions, but a man is primarily concerned with the "facts.". . . The average woman speaks nearly 25,000 words a day, while the average man speaks only around 12,500!

No husband will make perfect decisions or be without fault. But using a variety of ways to express genuine appreciation or admiration for your mate can keep him from looking to someone else to meet that need.

Treasuring is an attitude we carry in our hearts, a conviction we hold deep down inside. It's one big decision that plays itself out in 10,000 little decisions every day of our lives. This one giant choice to treasure your husband lights up a home like nothing else.

*A*s a wife, doing recreational things with your husband can be a key to keeping his interest. That doesn't mean you have to take up hunting or hang gliding, but picking an interest of his—and making it one you can share with him—can pay rich dividends.

*M*any men will do almost anything to gain the admiration of others. They will literally search for someone to love and respect them. Make sure that someone is you.

If you truly expect to have meaningful communication with your husband, you have to activate the right side of his brain so he can understand your feelings. One of the best ways to do this is with a word picture.

Become a channel of God's love to your husband. Jesus calls on you to love God with your whole heart and your neighbor (especially your husband) as you do yourself (see Matthew 22:37-40).

The more skilled a wife becomes in meeting her husband's legitimate needs, the more indispensable she is to him. Her act of serving in love builds her own security in the marriage.

Every man needs to know that someone, somewhere in the world, cares about him. He needs to feel warm, friendly acceptance from a committed, intimate friend who will be devoted to him no matter what he does. In other words, just like you, your husband needs the security of genuine love.

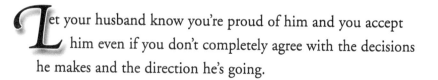

*L*et your husband know you're proud of him and you accept him even if you don't completely agree with the decisions he makes and the direction he's going.

*W*hen your husband is down, don't react with disgust as though he had lost his masculinity. Maintain the attitude that he's important.

When you've hurt your man's feelings, consider him valuable enough to admit you were wrong and ask for his forgiveness.

When your husband shares an idea with you that doesn't sit right, be careful how you respond. He needs the confidence and security of knowing you won't react in a severe or overly negative way.

*M*en need to know their advice is valuable. You welcome your husband's advice by . . .

- putting aside all other interests and giving him your full attention.
- focusing your eyes on him as he speaks.
- pointing out positive or helpful aspects of his advice.
- letting him have the floor until he has fully expressed his opinion.
- thanking him for the time he spent offering his advice.

*T*hough your husband may not demonstrate or even realize it, he needs you to teach him about intimate relationships! Men can learn how to relate at a deep level, but only when they've chosen to communicate—a decision you can help your mate to make.

*Y*ou can motivate your husband to love you by learning to be a courageous, persistent, and patient wife. As a completer and helper, you will need courage to help motivate change, gentle persistence to make sure it continues, and patience to wait on the Lord when change is long in coming.

*K*eep a mental list of little things your husband does that save you time and effort, and thank him for them as often as possible. When he feels he's meeting the "small" as well as the big needs of his family, his self-respect increases, and he will often begin to feel a deeper love for his appreciative wife.

Your husband needs to be made aware—in creative, loving ways—how to meet your needs. Remember, you're in the process of sharing with him how to love you, and he's in the process of learning. If you're on the same train, don't expect him to get to the destination before you do.

Men *need* to feel appreciated. Many husbands think their biggest contribution to you and the family is the financial support they provide. So one of the best ways to show your appreciation is to thank him for his faithfulness on the job. Even if you're providing part of the income (or most of it!), it's crucial that you show him how grateful you are for his provision.

A woman's native ability in the area of relationships is her greatest resource. With it, she can lovingly and persistently help her husband fulfill life's most important responsibilities and reach the most crucial biblical milestones in life.

*D*on't feel hurt and condemn your husband because he doesn't speak the "language of relationships" very well. To him, it's like a foreign language. Instead, help him learn to use it as fluently as you do.

By diminishing your expectations—by not expecting your husband to provide a level of fulfillment that only God can give—you free your husband of a burden you otherwise force him to bear, and you free yourself from unnecessary disappointment. This doesn't mean ignoring your needs or wants, just getting rid of your time limit and preconceived ideas about when and how those expectations will be met.

When your husband disciplines one of your children, avoid the temptation to criticize him in front of the child or defend the child's action that provoked his correction. The first step in developing a calm attitude is to *control* your tendency to overreact.

Never belittle your husband's job or the importance of his activities at work. Nothing destroys a man's self-esteem more than to hear his wife cutting down his efforts to support her. And remember that being ignorant of what he does on the job may, in his eyes, be the same as belittling his work.

Refrain from confronting your husband's deficiencies in anger. A man has a tendency to fight his conscience, and if you *become* his conscience, he'll either fight you or flee from you. Whichever route he takes, you've failed in your desire to spend more time with him.

*E*very man has tremendous value. It's hidden at times, perhaps, but always there—a worth based on the incredible impact he has on every member of the family through his everyday actions and attitudes. Encourage him to remember how important he is and to make that impact positive and affirming.

*L*ove grows out of an attitude of honoring someone. When we decide someone is valuable, that decision alone is a major first step in acting out our love for the person.

*M*ost men don't have all the "right brain" relational talents that most women do, but they can gain the knowledge and skills to become effective communicators. In fact, one of the strengths of men is that they can make a left-brain decision to develop those skills by asking probing questions (which is something they're good at).

*Y*our husband might sometimes irritate you, belittle you, offend you, ignore you, or even nauseate you, but admiration looks beyond what he does to who he is. It's unconditional. Men gravitate toward those who admire them.

A man's competitive nature, when turned toward gaining a successful relationship, can cause dramatic growth in his marriage. Once the knowledge and skills of good relationships are in sight, he can go after them the same way he "conquers" a project at work.

Y our husband will usually gain more intimacy from what he "does" with you than from what you the two of you talk about. So plan activities each week where you can bond by enjoying each other as you do something together.

Gary: A lot has been written and said about how to communicate in marriage. I should know—I've done my share of the talking in my previous books and seminars! But the fact is that it took me a long time to learn one of the most important communication skills—how to listen.

I especially needed to learn how to listen to Norma!

Norma: In the Bible, the book of Genesis says God made the wife to be her husband's completer—to give him strengths and insights he didn't have on his own. As Gary's work has developed over the years, I've tried to be that completer for him, but he hasn't always listened because I've often had to say things he didn't want to hear!

One of the areas where he didn't want to listen was the subject of how big and complex our ministry staff should (or shouldn't) become.

Gary: As the ministry began to really grow a number of years ago, with new opportunities opening up nearly every day, it seemed natural to me that our staff should expand to meet those demands. There were seminars to run, books to publish, film series to produce, small-group studies to develop, and so on.

I was ready to build an empire! I started interviewing and hiring people to help turn my dreams into reality.

Norma didn't think that was a good idea and told me so. I didn't agree and told *her* so. Before too long, however, events would prove she was right.

Norma: Gary is a wonderfully gifted man in so many ways. But one of those ways is *not* administration. Based on his natural strengths and weaknesses, I don't think God ever intended him to manage a large organization. There are other ministries and companies through which he can exercise his speaking and other gifts.

Nonetheless, as he said, he wouldn't hear that from me and so went about hiring people. Some of them lasted only six months before they would leave in frustration and disappointment.

Finally, though Gary still wasn't convinced I was right, he could see there were problems, so he agreed to seek some outside counsel. A short time later, we went to dinner with Dr. James Dobson, whose own Focus on the Family ministry was already fairly large and continuing to grow.

Gary: We met him in a restaurant there in Southern California. As soon as we were ready to get down to business, I told him, "Jim, I want a staff as big as yours," and I explained all the things I thought God was calling us to do.

"Well," he said, "let me ask you a few things." Then he asked a series of questions meant to reveal what kind of administrator I would be—things like "Are you good with details?" and "Can you make hard decisions and communicate them to your staff?"

As he posed those questions, I had to answer *no* to every one.

And all the time we were talking, Norma was kicking me under the table and smiling at me.

Norma: From talking with a lot of women, I know Gary was far from alone at that point in being willing to accept an insight from someone outside the family that he had been rejecting from his wife.

To his credit, Gary listened to Jim that day, and from that time forward we've kept our ministry staff small and done a lot of work through others, like book publishers and Promise Keepers. That experience was also a part of his learning process—learning to listen to me, even when he wanted to disagree, with the belief that I might have some helpful insight that he didn't possess.

Gary: It took me a lot of years, but eventually I accepted the fact that I had better listen carefully when Norma speaks about my strengths and gifts, about people and projects, and so on. She knows me better than I know myself in some ways, and she has a wonderful intuitive sense about people and situations.

As we look back on our time together now, we can see dozens and dozens of times when she has guided me, protected me, and kept me from doing foolish things. So no less than a hundred times, I've thanked her for going through the pain of speaking up through the years when she knew I wasn't going to like what she needed to say.

If you want *your* mate to be all the help to you that God intended, start today to really listen to—and take to heart—what he or she has to say.

*A*n emotional word picture is a communication tool that uses a story or object to activate simultaneously the *emotions* and the *intellect* of a person. In so doing, it causes the person to *experience* our words, not just hear them. A simple example of a word picture would be, "My week so far has made me feel like a puppy picked up by the scruff of its neck, because I feel carried along by circumstances beyond my control."

*T*he communication bridge between you and your spouse can be an emotional word picture, which can be a tremendous help in adding depth and impact to your conversations.

*T*here's more to effective communication than putting together and then practicing the right message. Picking the right *time* and *place* to convey it is also crucial.

*C*onsistent, gentle touching is a powerful way to increase feelings of security, prime the pump for meaningful communication, and set the stage for emotionally bonding and romantic times. That's because a gentle hug is a powerful *nonverbal word picture* of love.

*I*f a man is to be truly effective in his relationships both at home and at work, he needs to develop the ability to speak the "language of the heart" (facts *and* feelings). Right there under the same roof is a woman who can help him learn that skill.

*I*n a marriage, meaningful words bring life-giving water to the soil of a person's life. In fact, all loving relationships need the continual intake of the water of communication or they simply dry up. No marriage can survive without it.

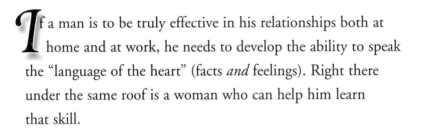

*H*ealthy communication is the lifeblood of love. A relationship will only be as good as its communication.

*P*eople who consistently use word pictures to point out the faults of others are misusing this communication method. They may make you feel terrible with their words and somehow convince you it's your fault. Word pictures are to be used to convey how you feel, not to attack the other person.

*A*n emotional word picture can help sharpen and extend your skills by maximizing your words. It also helps you whittle many problems down to size.

*H*ow do you honestly tell the one you love about something you find displeasing or aggravating without prompting that familiar defensive stare or indifferent shrug? You can help your mate become more sensitive to the problem by using a word picture rather than direct confrontation. Use examples that interest him or her, such as hobbies, everyday objects, or imaginary stories.

A lot of men avoid soft words and tender comfort because they've never been taught how to use them. Nor do they understand the positive effects those things will have on their wives and the sense of well-being they themselves will receive.

*E*xplain how you feel instead of demanding that your partner improve. Use "I feel" statements, but wait for the right time, and abandon the "you" statements and the "I told you so" statements.

*M*eaningful communication is sharing your feelings, goals, and ideas—your very personhood. But it isn't always easy to express those deeper things to one another. That's where a word picture can help to bring your thoughts to life, activating your mate's emotions as well as intellect.

*C*ommunication within the family is like the body's circulatory system. When we stop listening to each other, it's as though the family suffers a stroke. We become disabled. Certain members no longer respond to other members.

*I*n defeating the arguments and problems that can crop up around any home, try seasoning each day with a liberal sprinkling of praise: "I'm proud of you." "What a good helper!" "Way to go!" "You're very special to me." "What a treasure you are!" "That's so creative!" "I'm praying for you." "You're wonderful!" "I'm with you all the way."

*W*ithout meaning to, we can communicate nonverbally that other people or activities are more important to us than family. You've heard of football widows. How about golf orphans?

*H*ow quick we are to pick out the negative while ignoring five equally obvious positives! Unless we're careful, our body language and facial expressions will tend to minimize our praise while maximizing our criticisms. Make it your goal to praise your mate for something at least once each day.

*C*ommunication takes perseverance—and the very strength and courage of God's Spirit—to replace impatience, insensitivity, and self-preoccupation with loving communication patterns.

Words have awesome power to build us up or tear us down emotionally. Many people can clearly remember words of praise their parents spoke years ago. Others can remember negative, cutting words—in extraordinary detail.

Communicate humility. At times, some people act as if they know all the answers. It's important that we be willing to learn and grow.

O
ther approaches to criticism: Be soft—you can often say the hardest thing to someone, and he or she will receive it if you say it gently. Ask questions—help people discover for themselves what you're trying to say. Use word pictures.

T
hose who know us best provide the best correction. In particular, our mates, who were designed by God to complete us, are most sensitive to the areas in which we need help.

*I*t's crucial that a husband listen to his wife's correction. Through her, he can learn how to love her as Christ loves the church, so that their relationship will blossom into the mature marriage God designed.

*T*he salt principle is a method of gaining and holding a person's attention by arousing curiosity. It's a way to create a thirst for constructive conversation in which both you and your spouse can learn about each other's needs. First, identify the need or concern to be discussed, and then identify areas of high interest to the other person—areas you can tap into to pique interest.

*W*ork to avoid judgmental attitudes like "How stupid!" "Oh, no, that would never work" or "You'll never understand!" If you criticize your mate in a condescending manner, you're actually pushing him or her further away from you. No one enjoys being with a disrespectful person (Proverbs 21:19).

*O*ne of the easiest ways to reduce misunderstandings and communication friction is to share only a few thoughts with someone and then allow the person to repeat back what he or she thinks you said, much as would happen when you place an order at a fast food drive-through. This method will also improve your listening skills.

*A*dded benefits of drive-through talking: (a) Gives you a chance to fully understand what the other person is saying before you respond. This also prevents tuning out the other person while he or she is talking. (b) Validates the other person and his or her opinions. When you not only listen but also repeat back what someone says, you communicate that the person and his or her opinions are important to you and worth taking seriously.

*M*any people complain that their mate is strangely silent when they do something above and beyond the norm. We need to give praise and thanks to each other for special acts of kindness.

A couple cannot survive if one person always makes decisions independent of the other. It takes longer to make a decision if you insist on discussion that produces unity, but it removes the danger of hasty decisions that can cause a couple future problems in their marriage.

W e can minister words of encouragement or plant seeds of praise that can grow into mighty trees—pillars that uphold an entire life.

*M*any things have to happen if you're going to agree on major decisions. Norma and I have had to reason together for long periods in order to discover the reasons behind each other's perspectives.

*N*o one likes to be criticized. However, if you sandwich your criticism between two slices of sincere praise, you'll be amazed at the difference in your mate's reactions.

*T*he key to close-knit communication is to make conversations "safe"—where opinions, feelings, and needs can be treasured and valued.

Resolving Conflict and Dealing with Anger

Gary: Conflict is inevitable in any close relationship, including marriage. When you put together two people, male and female, from different backgrounds, with different customs and traditions, with varying expectations and dreams—disagreements are *going* to happen.

The key issue is how you're going to deal with them.

Norma: We've found that sometimes conflicts come to a head quickly, and sometimes they build up over a long period. In our case, one issue developed over 30 years, and only recently did we get it worked out.

The problem was that Gary started snoring, and it got worse as time went on. At first it was only irritating, even a little amusing. But as Gary's volume increased, my patience decreased!

After a while, I realized he might actually have a serious medical problem known as sleep apnea. He would literally stop breathing for a few seconds as he slept, then begin again with a start, waking himself up a little in the process.

As a result, neither one of us was getting much quality sleep.

Gary: Like a typical man, however, I didn't think the problem was all that serious. And I certainly was in no hurry to go to a doctor!

I had to acknowledge, however, that neither of us was sleeping very well, and that the lack of rest was making us both irritable. You're probably not honoring your mate too well, either, when you don't let her get a good night's sleep.

But what finally drove me to seek medical help was when Norma moved into a separate bedroom! She had reached the point where she thought that was the only way she could get a little rest at night.

I went to a sleep clinic, where they determined that I do, indeed, have sleep apnea. And they prescribed a breathing machine that forces air into my mouth and lungs while I sleep.

It has been incredible! The difference between "before" and "after" is like the difference between night and day. I find I now have far more energy, a better ability to concentrate, and much less irritability than before.

Best of all, I also have Norma sharing a bedroom with me again!

Norma: Our experience with Gary's sleep apnea has taught us a couple of things about marital conflict. First, if there's frequently or even constantly a level of friction or tension between you and your spouse, it may have a *physical* cause. So before you draw negative conclusions about each other's character or cooperativeness, look into that possibility.

Solving your conflict could take a whole different direction from what you now think is needed if there is, in fact, a physical problem. (And conditions like sleep apnea, hormonal imbalances, and high blood pressure are more widespread than most people realize.)

Second, when there is a conflict, we have to focus on the *problem* and look for solutions to it rather than focusing on the other person.

Before Gary finally went and got treatment for his sleep apnea, I'll admit there were times when I got upset with him for not taking appropriate action and so forcing me to live with his continued snoring. But most of the time, I was able to keep things in a more healthy perspective. His apnea was the problem, not Gary himself.

If I had let myself get mad at Gary about it too often, we might have ended up sleeping in different *houses*.

Gary: That brings up another point that can't be made too often: If a husband and wife are going to keep tangoing together for a lifetime, they simply *must* learn to give, ask for, and receive forgiveness.

We *will* hurt each other from time to time, sometimes on

purpose and sometimes without knowing it. If those injuries aren't forgiven, the spirit of the person who was hurt will close, making real intimacy next to impossible.

Because of living with me, Norma has had to become an expert at offering forgiveness!

Norma: Gary knows I've needed to be forgiven my share of the time, too. But I absolutely agree that a willingness to forgive and to seek forgiveness when needed is one of the most crucial foundation stones in any marriage.

*M*any family conflicts are caused by viewing another person's strengths as weaknesses. A clear view of what naturally motivates another person can open the door to greater compassion, patience, compromise, and caring.

*W*hen you boil down a lot of destructive arguments, what you often find is a simple lack of facts. The conflicts begin when an individual sees something that bothers him and then draws a conclusion. But what he *thinks* he sees may not be true at all. There's nothing new about this advice. James, the Lord's brother, wrote, "My dear brothers, take note of this: Everyone should be quick to listen, slow to speak and slow to become angry" (James 1:19, NIV).

Constant disagreement can only weaken a marriage relationship. That's probably why Paul emphasized having oneness of spirit and mind in the church. He likened the struggle for oneness to a team of athletes striving to reach the goal (see Philippians 1:27).

Gentleness (a willingness to decrease our lectures and increase our tender expressions of love) is a key to marital growth. Tenderness acts like a firebreak to an advancing, angry forest fire.

Clearly understanding our God-given temperaments brings to light common causes of family disharmony, provides handles for resolving long-standing friction in the home, dramatically increases our feelings of value for our loved ones and friends, and gives additional reasons to honor God.

There's no way to overcome our weaknesses without knowing our strengths. Why? Almost without exception, our weaknesses are a reflection of our strengths being pushed to an extreme.

*I*n relating to others, are you shifted to one extreme or the other? Are you camped in the far reaches of the hard-side life, easily issuing commands and criticism but not given to caring actions? Or do you rarely move beyond an unhealthy soft side, unwilling to confront someone to take the lead?

*T*he most insecure people are those who can't distance themselves from their loved ones enough to discipline them. Loving discipline may put a temporary emotional distance between people, but if we balance that hard-side correction with softness, we won't lose love. If anything, we'll enrich it.

When parents fail to say no, unwanted attitudes are allowed to take root in their homes. This builds learned helplessness and irresponsibility within kids. Such parents should be charged with delinquency of a minor.

How destructive bottled-up resentment can be! Anger has many tragic consequences in a marriage. It creates distance and pushes us into darkness. It can tie our emotions and decisions into knots.

We may not be able to keep anger from cropping up as an instantaneous and instinctive reaction to some pain or problem, but we can make a decision to keep it from staying in our lives and poisoning our attitudes or the attitudes of our loved ones.

We'll never be successful in our most important relationships until we learn to drain the anger out of another person's life.

*U*sually, by being soft, genuinely seeking to understand what happened, admitting when we're wrong, and specifically asking for forgiveness, we can see anger begin to drain away quickly in another.

*T*he buildup of unresolved anger results in a closed spirit. Selfish anger is the negative emotion we feel when a person or situation has failed to meet our needs, blocked our goals, or fallen short of our expectations. If you are constantly dishonoring your spouse for one reason or another, that will usually close his or her spirit.

*U*nresolved anger in your home is more toxic than the radon gas that seeps up from the earth and threatens many houses across the country.

*W*e may think people make us angry, but most of the time they simply reveal our own selfishness. What usually makes us angry is our lack of control over people and circumstances.

Survey after survey shows that the number one reason for mate selection is the *differences between* individuals. But differences can become a devastating source of conflict in a marriage. Learning to recognize and value each other's perspectives is one of the most positive things we can do.

As we attempt to open our spouse's spirit, our body language, muscles, facial expressions, and tone of voice must become soft, gentle, and caring. By doing this, we're saying that he or she is valuable, that we know something is wrong, and that we are open to listen.

When we have offended someone, we must give that person a chance to respond. *True restoration is confession of wrong* plus *forgiveness granted.*

Even when crises come from external sources, we must be careful not to close the spirits of those around us. When we are under stress, we can react harshly to our mate and close his or her spirit.

*A*nger is inevitable in a marriage. Couples who gain skills at "keeping their spirits open" to each other and at dealing with anger in a constructive way take giant strides toward intimacy.

*A*re you still hesitating to knock down old walls of anger and put in a doorway of tenderness to your home— a door that opens to energizing words, gentle touching, and courageous forgiving?

Deep-seated problems don't vanish instantly. They require consistent work by the couple and a reliance on God's strength for daily endurance.

Those men and women who are wise enough to reopen a person's spirit have to learn to listen beyond the words to the hurt feelings behind them.

*B*ecause a woman's need for a close, meaningful relationship is often greater than a man's, she is more sensitive to words and actions that can weaken a relationship.

*T*here are five keys or attitudes that open a closed spirit:

- Become gentle; demonstrate tenderheartedness.
- Understand what the other person has gone through, listening carefully not only to what is said, but also to how it is said. What has caused the anger?
- Acknowledge that the person is hurting, and admit when you have been offensive.
- Touch the other person gently.
- Ask for forgiveness.

Keeping our "heads together" in stressful times is something like a foxhole experience. Those who have endured the horrors of trench warfare often remain friends for life, even though their ordeal may have lasted only a few weeks or months. Why? Because shared experience, whether pleasant or unpleasant, creates the common ground in which deep-rooted relationships germinate and grow. The greater the intensity of the experience, the greater the potential for bonds of love and intimacy that can bind us to one another in a beautiful relationship called a close-knit family.

Do not be threatened by the presence of conflict, but use it as a flashing road sign that gets your attention to do whatever is necessary to resolve it at some point.

*A*nger creates distance, and distance destroys relationships. It causes husbands and wives and parents and children to drift away from each other. Home becomes little more than a dormitory with hostile roommates.

*N*o matter how hard we work at the relational "glue" that bonds our families together, anger is like fingernail polish remover that instantly dissolves that bonding.

*T*he issue" is the first level of conflict. If two disputing parties can keep talking on the issue level, discussing the merits of each position and thinking through possible compromises, the tension could actually be constructive rather than destructive.

*L*ike few other emotions, anger restricts and binds us, tying us in eternal knots. Forgiveness, on the other hand, sets us free from those bonds, untying the knots that hold us captive. The Lord Jesus said, "Forgive, and you will be forgiven" (Luke 6:37, NIV).

A couple in crisis sought out correction. It was difficult at first, and humbling. Yet what was that small discomfort and embarrassment compared to the years of love, companionship, and happy memories they will share for the rest of their lives? *Only the wise seek correction.*

Y ou can't schedule shared family crisis, but you can—and must—make sure family activities get high priority on your yearly schedule.

*T*here are five main reasons for conflict in the average relationship. *Power and control:* When both parties are fighting for control or resenting not being able to take control, there's conflict. *Individuality:* When one person tries to change or manipulate his or her partner, and the other resists, there's conflict. *Distance:* When one person begins pulling away or putting up walls and defenses, he or she begins to distrust, and the need for self-preservation arises. *Distrust:* When one or both people feel unsafe expressing their feelings or needs, there's conflict. *Unmet needs:* When one partner feels his or her needs are not being met, again there's conflict.

*T*he best way to handle conflict is to remain free of anger and blame and full of love and understanding.

Increasing Your Intimacy 100 Percent

Gary: When we say the word *intimacy,* most people immediately think of sex. But the physical act of coming together in marriage is only one aspect of intimacy. And in some ways, it's not even the most important aspect. (I know, you may find it hard to believe that a guy is saying that seriously, but hear me out.)

The real definition of intimacy between two people is that they feel safe enough with each other to share their feelings and needs. If a husband and wife have *that* kind of intimacy, they won't have much trouble with sexual intimacy (unless, of course, there's a physical problem).

Norma: Going by that definition of intimacy, I have to say that we really didn't have it for the first 20 years of our marriage. It took me that long to realize the importance of sharing my feelings *and* to feel safe enough to do it.

For example, when we got married, I moved to Gary's town and started attending his big church. We were surrounded by "his people." I wanted them to see clearly that he really cared for me. But he never showed me any affection in public.

It was frustrating and disappointing, yet I didn't say anything. Partly that was because I thought *That's just the way he is,* and partly I thought he should just *know* I was hurting—it seemed so obvious to me.

Gary: There's a good lesson for us men in that, since we're the ones who most often are cool toward our mates in public. Namely, we can simply ask our wives, "What would you like me to do to show publicly that I love you?"

And wives, if your husband *doesn't* ask that question or just isn't doing what you'd like (even if it's only holding hands as you walk together), please take the initiative to *tell* him—in a loving and gentle way, of course. Please *don't* expect him to read your mind!

Norma: I'm reminded of another thing we've learned that can greatly increase marital intimacy. In our case, I would say it has doubled it!

I used to get real excited when Gary would be asked to speak on a cruise, at a beach resort, or at some other nice vacation-type spot, and I was invited to go along. My thought would be that when he wasn't speaking, this would be a romantic, intimate getaway for the two of us.

But I never told Gary that was my expectation. Again, I thought he should just know.

Then, what happened *every* time was that about two days into the trip, Gary would want to start talking about setting goals and solving problems. I would be crushed, my dream shattered. Then I would withdraw from him physically and emotionally, because I knew that kind of discussion would be long and intense.

Gary: We'll talk in the next section about a couple of the things that have helped to develop more of a sense of security in our relationship. But one thing we've learned about how to increase intimacy in a situation like those trips is to simply agree beforehand on what we will and won't discuss.

Like us in the past, couples often use a date to catch up on issues and concerns between them. That's almost certain to *escalate* arguments rather than resolve them. Fortunately, I finally figured that out.

Norma: A woman equates "date" with "intimacy," which is why she looks forward to it so much. But when the conversation turns to dealing with issues instead, it kills that feeling and ruins the evening as far as she's concerned.

What a simple thing it is to have an agreement before a date or a special vacation about what you will and won't talk about! Yet I can say without hesitation that it has increased our intimacy, and our enjoyment of those times together, by at least 100 percent.

Give it a try in your marriage!

*I*t's crucial that we develop healthy relationships. Doctors have found that tension from a poor marriage or friendship can actually cause illness and shorten a person's life! Not only that, but our children also gain or suffer from the model we provide them every day.

*H*ere are some overall ways of building intimacy: Stop waiting for things to get better; make a decision to work on them. Acquire and practice new attitudes and skills that lead to fulfilling relationships. Commit to changing your own behaviors first, without expecting your partner to change his or hers. Support each other in your efforts so that neither of you feels alone or inferior.

*O*ne of the keys in any healthy relationship is a willingness to say, "I'm more interested in understanding what you're saying than in thinking of what I'm going to say once you're done talking."

A husband and wife need to establish a routine pattern of meaningful communication—times of sharing feelings, hopes, dreams, and fears. "Weather report" comments like "How's it going?" "How was the traffic today?" and other safe questions aren't enough. Every day, spouses need to add the water of well-spoken words to keep their relationship strong and healthy.

A marriage can't be sustained with romance alone. But added to security, meaningful communication, and meaningful touch, it can be a tremendous source of energy and growth.

*W*ise husbands and wives will take time to practice small acts of touching: Holding hands in a walk through the mall, stopping to rub your mate's shoulders for a moment, taking the time to gently hold your spouse at the door on your way out. These small but important acts can work like "superbloom" to a plant and green out a relationship.

*I*n a nurturing and healthy relationship, you perceive that your ideas and insights are valuable, and you learn how to negotiate and listen to the other person's views. You hear things like "What a great idea!" "What do you think about this?" and "Your opinion means so much to me."

*W*hen your spouse seeks to honor you, you're listened to and encouraged to participate in discussions and decisions. You hear things like "What did you say?" "You always know the right thing to say," or "Let's talk about this."

*I*n a healthy relationship, not only are you encouraged to feel, but you're also sensitive to others' feelings. You perceive that how you feel is valuable and that you're safe when sharing your feelings. You might hear things like "How do you feel about this?" "It's okay to feel like that," or "What can I do to make you feel better?"

*W*hen you honor your spouse above yourself, you develop close-knit feelings of belonging. In this atmosphere, you spend a great deal of quality time together. You might hear things like "Let's spend some time together," "What can I do to become closer to you?" or "What can I do to make you feel closer to me?"

*C*ommunication is the single most effective way to deepen intimacy in any relationship, whether it's with your mate, family, friends, or on the job. Just as food is essential to a healthy body, intimate communication is essential to a healthy relationship.

*W*hat are the five levels of communication? 1. *Clichés:* "How's it going?" or "What's up?" 2. *Facts:* "Looks like rain today" or "Sure is hot out." 3. *Opinions:* "I think the Raiders are going to win the Super Bowl" or "Your mother is interfering." 4. *Feelings:* "How do you feel about this?" or "I love you." 5. *Needs:* "What do you need to be happy?" or "I really need a hug from you."

*G*enerally, our communication is based on what we consider to be within our safety zone. It's incredibly safe to exist on clichés or by simply stating facts. Most conflicts begin to enter into the picture when we share opinions, feelings, or needs.

*T*he most successful relationships are those in which each person feels safe sharing his or her *feelings* and *needs*. This is where our personalities and parenting histories strongly affect us, because many of us are fearful or uncomfortable about sharing such intimacies.

When you go to a restaurant, you request items off a menu. The same principle can be applied to a relationship. Request what you want from your mate—for example, a daily hug, help around the house, or appreciation for a job well done. Decide what's most important in your marriage, and put those things in writing.

One menu item I suggest you include is an agreement that during an argument, you'll both list all the positive and negative aspects of the issue at hand. Seeing both sides can bring about a quicker resolution and also the unity you both desire.

Life is more predictable—more secure and stable—when you know that both of you are working toward a loving, lasting relationship. This is the foundation for true intimacy.

*W*hen you and your spouse agree to live in oneness, you're consequently willing to spend more time listening and discussing in order to resolve important issues and so build intimacy.

*W*henever a husband and wife agree on the main areas of their lives, they become bonded together and achieve a unique strength. Desert Storm was a military success because the various leaders battled with a clearly understood plan and mutual strategy. *Two people united are much stronger than one.*

Keeping your written relationship menu posted in a prominent household location provides a continual reminder of which values and rules you're working toward. It generally takes about 30 days to start a new habit. So if you're regularly working on attaining your goals, it will only take a month before you notice significant changes in your relationship.

One important way to build intimacy is to give frequent praise. The simplest way to make your spouse feel good is to say, "Well done!"

Many men don't realize it, but more than 80 percent of a woman's need for meaningful touch is nonsexual. Sex does not begin in the bedroom. It actually starts in the everyday acts of truthfulness, consistency, kindness, touching, and talking that build a growing desire in a woman.

Genuine love doesn't necessarily spring from feelings. Its basis is primarily a concern for the welfare of another. Although the feelings of affection will follow, genuine love is initially an action directed toward fulfilling another person's needs.

*N*o one can continually ignore considerate, loving actions. If you make your mate feel special, you increase his or her desire to do the same for you.

*P*ersistent love—like the dripping of water on a rock—can wear away a person's resistance. It's nearly impossible to stay angry with or emotionally distant from someone who unconditionally loves and values you.

*O*ne of the greatest secrets in history is that true happiness comes from reaching out to others with a genuine desire for them to feel love from us.

*O*ne way to cherish our mates is to help them become fulfilled as people. We can do this by discovering their personal goals and looking for ways to help them reach those objectives. We all love to know someone is pulling for us.

From time to time, my wife and I get together on a date, for breakfast out or just a retreat from home. During that time, we list our personal goals and commit ourselves to helping each other fulfill those desires. I feel so satisfied knowing that my wife is committed enough to sacrifice for my goals and that I have the same commitment toward her.

So many men and women treat each other as objects to be used. They may not verbalize it, but they maintain an inward conviction that their mate should do things that have never been discussed. This is like steadily pouring acid on intimacy.

*W*e should instead discuss our roles in marriage and what areas we can encourage each other to do. We should choose areas based on genuine love and not on expectations that have never been discussed.

*O*ne way intimacy is blocked is when our lives are filled with unhealthy behavior—habits and addictions that affect our daily conduct. To change those habits and addictions, we should first recognize our mistakes and admit when we're at fault. Second, we must keep an attitude of wanting to improve. Third, we should share our feelings and needs with our mate and seek his or her understanding and support.

Keeping Alive Romance and Security

Gary: In this day and age, security in the marriage relationship almost seems to have gone the way of the dodo. Roughly half of all marriages end in divorce, and the statistics are about the same among Christians as they are in society at large.

Yet feeling secure in the relationship is vital to true romance. How can you give yourself fully and without reservation to your spouse unless you're confident he or she will still be with you, loving and supporting you, next week, next year, 10 years from now, and so on until the day that death finally separates you?

Norma: One way I've tried to build security in our marriage is that I've consciously and deliberately never used the words *hate* or *divorce* or *leave* with Gary, even in our most heated "discussions." I'll admit I *thought* the words on a number of occasions in years gone by. But I've seen the devastation done to individuals—men and women as well as children—and families by separation and divorce, and I never wanted any part of that.

Even more, when I vowed on our wedding day to love and remain faithful to Gary, I was making that promise to God. I was making it to Gary as well, but I was especially making it to God, and I take that very seriously.

Gary: Another thing that has helped to build security in our relationship is that *we pray together* about anything in our family or ministry that looks challenging. There's a great sense of peace and oneness that comes from going to God together and placing a difficult matter in His hands.

We also know that when we're both seeking His will for a particular concern, we're on the right track to finding a good answer, because self-centeredness and ego have been taken out of play. We both want what's best for each other, for our marriage, for our family, or whatever the case may be.

Norma: It's nice to get flowers and to go out for fancy dinners. Those kinds of things do develop the feelings of romance that are so enjoyable, and I certainly like it when they're a part of our relationship.

I've learned, however, that as nice as the feelings of romance are, they're no substitute for the security of a rock-solid commitment. Knowing that your love and your marriage will truly last "till death do us part" is the greatest feeling of all!

During hard times, when I don't *feel* love toward Gary, I always remember that feelings change so many times during the day because situations change—but my decision to love him was a commitment for life.

These are the four elements of marital intimacy:
• *Unconditional security,* a lifetime commitment to caring for someone. • *Meaningful communication,* daily sharing your feelings, needs, hopes, and dreams (and being a good listener when the other person speaks). • *Romantic experiences,* setting your schedule to include intimate times together rather than letting the pressures of life set your schedule for you. • *Intimate touch,* since 8 to 10 loving touches a day keep the marriage counselor away!

A marriage needs security to grow and thrive. To use a different analogy, the first structural support that holds up a meaningful relationship is found in that one word—*security*.

Security is the assurance that someone is committed to loving and valuing us for a lifetime. It's a constant awareness that whatever difficulties we face, we'll work to overcome them together.

Security means we're fully committed to the truth and make a decision daily to be open to correction. We build security into our relationship each time we speak the truth, go out of our way to encourage our spouse, listen without lecturing, or give him or her a gentle hug.

A gardener—nurturer—has a responsibility not only to find out what's wrong with a plant, but also to do whatever is necessary to nurse it back to health. In Ephesians 5:21-33, we see this picture as a role of the husband.

E very enduring marriage involves an unconditional commitment to an imperfect person—your spouse.

A key to blending friendship with romance is to take the time to explore each other's interests and then share in them.

A character of honesty and serving must be deep-rooted to survive; it reaches way down into the soil of consistent living. It isn't a short-term change of behavior that makes an impression on your mate; *it's a life*.

*I*f you want to raise the passion level in your marriage, increase the purity of your character.

*C*onversely, all it takes to see the romantic spark doused with buckets of cold water is to expose major impurities in one's character.

Couples need to create emotional bonding times. Keeping the flames of romance alive may not seem as important as security or meaningful communication, but it is. Consistent positive times of emotional bonding can add tremendous stability to a home.

A man will do almost anything to gain the admiration of others. The most important person from whom he wants it is his wife. Some women think that because their husbands are admired by others in their professions, they don't need it from their wives. That's a serious mistake.

*A*s leaders in their homes, men need to find out how their wives like to be touched, how often, when, and where.

*W*hen you speak of a man's personal power, you immediately think of words reflecting character like *warmth, sensitivity, dependability, determination, genuine compassion,* and *caring.*

*T*ouch has the power to instantly calm, reassure, transfer courage, and stabilize a situation beginning to spin out of control. With touch, we push back the threatening shadows of anger, bitterness, loneliness, and insecurity.

*R*emaining tender during a trial is one of the most powerful ways to build an intimate relationship (James 1:19-20).

ake the initiative occasionally to suggest a specific time to talk together. For example, set up a breakfast or dinner out with just the two of you. Let your convictions show. Meaningful conversation is crucial in developing a growing and loving relationship.

ow can we turn our negative thoughts to positive ones before they affect our sense of worth and become a hurtful part of our self-image? By developing a grateful attitude. One of the most attractive qualities a person can have is a spirit of gratefulness.

Once a man can see the advantages in making a choice (the facts), he can often commit himself regardless of his feelings. For instance, even on a day when he doesn't necessarily "feel" like doing something (like spending a half hour in meaningful conversation with his wife), he can still make a decision to do so.

Romance is the process of keeping your courtship alive long after the wedding day.

Romantic touching and hugging can convey peace and comfort, as well as love. To the degree that we employ it with our mate, we remove the emotional threats that block intimacy.

Meaningful touching outside the bedroom can create sparks in a marriage, and meaningful communication can fan the flames.

*D*esign togetherness times that incorporate your spouse's interests. These may involve athletic events, musical concerts, museum trips, meals out, fine arts and entertainment, vacations, and so on.

*M*ost women report that they *need* to feel emotionally connected to enjoy physical intimacy. They need to feel loved and cherished. They need displays of physical affection, but not necessarily the sex act itself. Men, however, are motivated by the sexual act. They *need* sexual intimacy and state that physical affection and feeling cherished aren't always necessary for them to feel sexually satisfied. However, men still need affection and cherishing in the overall relationship.

When used correctly, the differences in the way men and women respond to sex can complement each other. When not taken into consideration, these differences will tear apart the very fabric of your mutual fulfillment.

Decide to stop waiting for things to get better. Only the two of you working together toward love will make the intimate difference. Acquire and practice new attitudes and skills that lead to fulfilling relationships.

The key to a close-knit marriage is maximizing the times together and minimizing the times apart. Our culture has a tendency to emphasize "doing your own thing" rather than marital closeness. The more activities you can do as a couple, the better are the chances that you'll develop a deep, lasting relationship.

What increases security in a marriage?

- Saying "I love you" regularly.
- Making long-range plans together.
- Cultivating a pattern of thoughtfulness.
- Valuing each other's thoughts and feelings.
- Demonstrating a strong commitment to Christ and to the spiritual health of your family.

In marriage, providing a deep sense of security for your partner is like bathing him or her in warm sunlight. That means convincing your mate in a variety of ways that, no matter what, you'll always be there to care for him or her.

*C*an you imagine the ecstatic feeling you would have if your mate volunteered the question, "How can I become a better mate?" The honor you would feel would be overwhelming. So how about asking the question yourself?

*W*ives tell me they admire and honor a husband who admits he's wrong, especially when he openly seeks his wife's advice on how to improve. Many a husband has refused to listen to his wife's correction because of hang-ups over her choice of words.

*P*romise yourself to tell your mate daily what you appreciate about him or her. People love encouraging notes or special gifts. Praise your mate in a way you know he or she will enjoy.

*O*ne husband praised his wife by taking 365 pieces of candy and writing a praise on every wrapper. She opened one piece every day for a full year.

Finding Treasures in Trials

Gary: One of the most helpful life skills I've ever learned is what I call treasure-hunting trials, or finding treasures in trials. The concept is simple, though doing it can be hard, especially at first. But once you've made a habit of it, the benefits are incredible.

In a nutshell (I spend a lot of time developing the concept in my seminar and some of my later books), the idea is that even in trying times and circumstances, we can find some redeeming good if we'll just look for it. No matter how bad a situation may be, there's something worthwhile to be discovered.

This concept has been enormously helpful not only to Norma and me, but it has also helped—in some cases revolutionized the lives of—many people with whom I've counseled.

Norma: Since learning how to do this, treasure-hunting trials has become an emotional and spiritual life raft for me. For example, when Gary does something to offend me (often without even realizing it) and doesn't seek my forgiveness, it's easy for me to feel hurt and discouraged. When that happens, however, I've learned to deal with it, with the Lord's help.

First, I take a few minutes to thank Him for Gary and for the situation. I can do that sincerely—even though I don't *feel* thankful yet—because I know God put us together. I also know from experience that Gary's intentions toward me are basically good and honoring.

Second, because I'm confident that I *will* be able to find good in the circumstance if I just look for it, I ask myself, "What's one neat thing I'm learning because of the situation I'm in?" When I take the time to think that way and do a little digging, I always do find *at least* one good thing in that trial.

The treasure I find may be patience, greater compassion for others, a better understanding of how to get along with Gary, or something else. But whatever it is, it's always an insight or a strength that I'm glad to have in my life.

On those rare occasions when Gary is down emotionally because of a difficulty, I'm even able to help him sometimes by getting him started on his own treasure-hunting.

Gary: I remember a time not long ago when I was really bothered by something, and treasure-hunting again proved to be a great help.

There's a strong history of heart trouble among the men in my family—both my father and a brother died relatively young of heart attacks. For a long time, I ignored the implications of that for myself. I didn't exercise, and I ate whatever I wanted, whenever I wanted it. Finally, a few years ago, a doctor convinced me that I had to start taking better care of myself, and I became a "convert" to regular exercise and healthful eating.

Well, when I learn something or become convinced of something, I want everyone else to get on board as well! So when I became more health-conscious, I also thought Norma should start taking better care of *herself*—exercising, eating right, drinking lots of water, and so on.

Norma: When Gary does something like this, he becomes a fanatic! In front of a seminar audience, he comes across as highly motivating about whatever he believes in. But at home, he can be pushy and controlling. That makes me want to *resist* rather than get on board with him.

Gary: That's exactly what happened in this case. I didn't think she was as concerned about her health as she should be, so I started pushing, and she immediately started resisting. It became a point of contention and argument between us.

This went on for several years, and I prayed about it every day. (Mostly I prayed that God would change Norma's mind.) Finally, although I was still concerned that she wasn't taking very good care of herself, I realized that my badgering wasn't doing any good, so I made a commitment to stop trying to "motivate" her. I decided I would leave the matter of how she cared for herself physically to her and God.

I thought of this as a trial because I was as concerned about her as ever, and she wasn't doing any of the things yet that I thought she should. So I asked the Lord, "Where's the treasure in this, God? What good *has* come or *will* come out of this situation?"

To my surprise, not long after I made that commitment, Norma started doing some of what I had hoped for all along to take better care of herself! For example, she started drinking a lot more water, which is a simple yet very healthful thing to do.

Norma: When Gary quit trying to be the Holy Spirit in my life in that area, telling me what I should and shouldn't do, I quit resisting. I actually gave some thought to what he had been saying for years, and I realized I could do some good things for myself without making radical changes in my lifestyle.

Gary: Out of that whole experience, I actually got two unexpected treasures. First, of course, Norma started doing some of the things that make for better health. That's a treasure to me not because she was finally doing what I wanted her to do, but because I want to enjoy her company for as long as possible, and her new habits should help to increase that time.

Second, I got the treasure of watching *God* work things out that I never could have made happen myself. And in the process, I developed a greater trust in Him and in the power of prayer.

Now, that's a treasure worth cherishing!

"Treasure hunting" (looking for gold in every trial or guilt experience) can help us form a genuine love or deeper sensitivity toward others who are hurting in a similar way. It can also help us forgive those who have wronged us and cause us to be less judgmental or critical, leading us to the door of God's grace.

No one likes trials, yet no one can escape them. We can let them ruin our lives—making us bitter, angry, and resentful—or we can look for the treasure that will let us love and serve others.

Steps involved in treasure hunting: 1. Recognize the pain you've experienced—don't deny the anger and hurt. 2. When it's called for, go through a grieving period. 3. During the midst of a trial, hang on to the hand of God. Concentrate on keeping your eyes and expectations focused on Him. 4. Wait expectantly on the Lord, like a child on Christmas morning, to bring to light the gold, blessing, or benefits that come from the trials you're experiencing. 5. Use the extra sensitivity, compassion, endurance, or wisdom you've gained from a trial to help others.

We can thank God during our difficult circumstances because we know love is hidden in the pain.

We'll catch the true meaning of Christ's teaching on faith if we pay attention to how He helped distraught people through their trials. Many of us make the mistake of forgetting that Jesus promises to produce maturity, righteousness, and love by letting us go through trials.

God's best and highest will is for us to love (value) Him with all our hearts, and to love (value) others as ourselves. Do you realize you have everything you need to fulfill God's will and experience His best in your life?

Sometimes the treasure is coated with corrosion, but if we do some scraping, we begin to see its value. Thanksgiving expresses our faith that God can, indeed, bring treasures out of trials, and faith adds muscle to the scraping process, even in the worst of trials.

Whenever I feel fear or worry, I thank the Lord for the feeling, then test the following six reasons until I understand the source: the future, my reputation, money, possessions, time, or health. After that, I submit the concern to Him.

*E*very problem—great or small—has in it a treasure waiting to be discovered. The secret to successful treasure hunting is understanding two life-changing words: *faith* and *love*.

*A*nger, hurt feelings, fear, and lust can actually help us develop a closer, more vital relationship with Jesus by serving as warning signals.

*A*lmost every trial increases our love for others. So even if we don't see any other good, we know of at least one—more love.

*K*eep a watchful eye on your mate's responses during a trial. A few days after a trial, look for an opportunity to discuss how God could use it in his or her life.

During difficult times, it's vital not to do or say anything that will close the spirit of your spouse. Harsh words and callous actions in the heat of battle are the quickest way to dilute the "glue" of bonding.

Great faith is the confidence, even *during* a trial, that it will one day turn out to be to our benefit. "Dinky" faith is complaining or "murmuring" during a trial that there will be no benefit.

The real secret to becoming a close-knit couple is shared experiences that turn into shared trials.

Though trouble may look at the time as if it's destroying your home, it can actually turn into a benefit through God's power!

Being neck-deep in a crisis doesn't find us saying, "Isn't this great?" Normally it gets tense, and we choke back words of anger and frustration. The secret is how we'll feel later. In most cases, it takes a couple of weeks for the "glue" of a shared predicament to set in place.

Disappointed expectations confront us all. *How we handle those disappointments will have a powerful impact on the peace and stability of our lives.*

*L*ife's game plan includes some changes you can anticipate and plan on. But it will also be filled with sneaky speed bumps, strange detours, frustrating dead ends, sudden lane changes, and unscheduled exits. If you anticipate both the major "expected" changes as well as probable unexpected changes, you'll stand a better chance of reaching your destination . . . together.

*W*hen we're hit with one of life's trials, we often overreact and panic. Before you tell yourself that this is a major disaster, take a few minutes to figure out what has transpired, assessing the actual damage. Remember, nothing is ever as bad as it seems at first glance.

*A*void continual concentration on what you're losing or being denied in a trial. Try to think of what new opportunities this situation may bring, what you might learn from this obstacle, and what future happiness lies in store.

*A*void the *blame* game. Don't beat yourself up over mistakes you've made or personal losses or mistreatment you might have received. If you can avoid shame and blame, your recovery will be much quicker.

*A*llow yourself to grieve over any pain from discomforting experiences. Though I urge you to keep an optimistic outlook when confronted with a negative experience, it's still important to allow yourself to figure out what took place, analyze how it makes you feel, and sense the pain associated with the event. If you don't take this step, you can fall into denial and stuff the feelings so deep that you think you've solved the problem.

*B*egin to treasure hunt as soon as possible and as long as you're able. This isn't something you do for just a short time after a trial; you continue doing it until your thinking actually changes and you realize the positive results of your positive thinking. You'll have a victory over your pain when you see the benefits of the event and have feelings of greater love and self-worth.

Whenever we're hit with a trial, if we don't allow ourselves to become angry and bitter, we'll become much more empathetic toward others who are experiencing similar problems and more sensitive to their feelings. All these things make us more loving and a better friend.

The pain we feel for others helps us move forward in our personal journey into maturity. Additional benefits include heightened thoughtfulness, gentleness, carefulness, kindness, patience, and self-control.

*D*on't allow guilt to overwhelm you when you notice negative emotional signals flashing. Rather, make a decision to use those signals as a motivation to evaluate and change your focus.

*T*reasure hunting is transforming *bitter* into *better*. When you're bitter, you're angry and feel low self-worth. When you're better, you feel grateful and enjoy an elevated sense of self-esteem.

One method I use to discover the treasure in my personal trials is to write on a piece of paper a list of my past trials and what possible benefits have come from each of them.

In the midst of our trials, God has designed a number of "home lightening" options that will bring warmth, brilliance, and beauty into our family rooms, dining rooms, bedrooms, and playrooms—bright lamps like unconditional affirmation, meaningful touch, hard-earned wisdom, unquestioned character, and spiritual dependence on Him.

*W*henever you begin to feel fear or worry, thank the Lord for the feeling. Then look at what might be causing it. Is it related to your future expectations? Is it your reputation? If you know which area has caused the fear or worry, present that to God as a confession of your need to trust Him to take care of the results.

*T*hree thoughts will help anyone facing a major transition in life: *Let go, start fresh,* and *reach out.*

*F*inding benefits in a trial may not come until months after it's over. But when you feel you can, here are some elements that can be discovered within any negative situation: *Self-appreciation*. List things you like about yourself. *Support system*. List the people who have helped you through your more serious trials. *Increased love*. List the ways the trial has helped you understand and care about others.

*W*hen you begin to treasure hunt *past* trials in your life, you'll develop a greater freedom from the pain that may still be affecting you. Anger will begin to evaporate, and areas of intimacy will open up.

Honoring God

Gary: Although this is the last section in the book, it's really the most important. That's because the tango of a satisfying marriage is most likely to occur when we put God at the center of the relationship and commit our lives to Him, both individually and as a couple.

One of the ways we do that, as I mentioned earlier, is that Norma and I pray together about anything and everything that looks difficult or challenging in our relationship, our family, or our ministry. In doing so, we acknowledge that He's our Lord, that we need His guidance, and that without His strength we won't succeed.

We also honor Him in that we never give up hope that He can fix whatever's wrong in our marriage (or any other area of need)—that He can do something supernatural to work things together for good. We know that He, in turn, will honor His Word in James 1:5-6 and give us the wisdom we need when we ask for it in faith.

Norma: I remember a time, years ago, when I had to make a very difficult choice if I was going to honor God in our marriage. Our finances were in deep trouble then, and I was the family book-keeper and bill payer. Gary was not the most responsible person in handling money, so I really didn't trust him in that area.

Then I heard a message in which the speaker said the husband ought to handle a couple's finances, and I was convicted by it. Now, neither Gary nor I necessarily agrees that the husband should *always* handle the finances, and we don't believe the Bible teaches it. Generally, whichever spouse is best at doing it should have the job. And today, I manage that area for both our family and our ministry.

At that time, however, the issue before me wasn't which of us could handle the checkbook better. It was, "Since I believe God is asking me to give this area over to Gary as a matter of obedience to Him, do I trust Him enough to do it? I can't trust Gary at this point, but will I trust God?"

Gary: When Norma says I wasn't responsible back then, she's putting the case charitably. From a logical perspective, it made no sense to hand our financial affairs over to me. Apart from God's intervention, she had every reason to expect that obeying Him would lead to disaster.

Norma: In spite of the danger, however, I was convinced that this was what God wanted me to do. And so it became a simple matter: Did I trust Him, and would I obey Him?

It wasn't an easy choice, but finally I decided that I did and I would.

I'm happy to report that God did intervene, and Gary grew tremendously in his ability to handle our finances responsibly. It didn't happen overnight, and that can be a difficult thing, because we tend to want God to make everything better right away. But over a period of many months, Gary "grew up" far more than I could have even hoped and became extremely responsible, to the point where I really could trust him in this area.

Today, when I tell this story to an audience, women will come to me afterward and say, "I couldn't do what you did." But to my mind, it was a matter of honoring God and obeying Him when I sensed His clear direction.

So my question to those women, and to you who are reading this book, is simply this: How much do you trust God?

Gary: Our purpose here isn't to preach at anyone. But we will say that in our experience, we have never been disappointed when we've put our trust in God. And our marriage is much the stronger as a result.

We've been tangoing together for more than 30 years now, and the "dance" keeps getting better every day. We pray the same will be true for you and your mate.

God's Word contains the only genuine blueprint for successful relationships, both with Him and with others.

If your focus strays from depending on Christ for strength and creativity, you may find yourself nagging your spouse. Anger and nagging usually stem from feelings of frustration at failing to change another person. While these "helpful reminders" may come from a sincere desire to help, actually, they *demotivate* a person and are a constant weight on him. Depending on God to change another person, rather than on ourselves, can have powerful results in a relationship.

*I*mportant Biblical Convictions in Marriage:

- Having a loving relationship with my spouse and children (see Ephesians 5:21-33).

- Spending quality time alone with my spouse and together with my family (following Christ's example of being alone with His disciples).

- Not allowing unresolved hurts to come between us; being tenderhearted and forgiving each other (see Ephesians 4:32).

- Honoring, or "blessing," each other (see Ephesians 5:33; 1 Peter 3:7).

- Expressing appreciation and minimizing a critical attitude toward each other (see 1 Corinthians 13:5-6).

- Endeavoring to be united in mind, spirit, and flesh (see Ephesians 5:31; Philippians 1:27; 2:2-3).

- Being committed to care unconditionally for my family.

*W*e know Christ is at the center of our relationships with others when negative emotions such as anger, hurt feelings, lust, and worry no longer control our lives.

*W*hen Christ is in control, our negative emotions are replaced by an inner contentment and love that come only from Him.

s I seek God daily, making sure I have His desires and believe Him for those desires, I can be assured of one thing—He answers the persistent prayers of His children. This is as true relative to our marriages as it is relative to any other area of life.

od's grace is power in us to control our tongue, even in heated discussions with a spouse, but He only gives grace to the humble. If we humble ourselves in His presence, recognizing our complete dependence on Him, He will exalt us.

God truly modeled the principles of touching when Jesus walked the back trails and highways of planet earth. No longer could God be thought of as some distant, unconcerned deity in a far corner of infinity. He came, robed in warm, human flesh. And while He walked among us, He reached out His hands.

Whatever your goals and ambitions for improving your marriage, you must learn the necessary skills, even though it may take years. Don't limit yourself and God by dwelling on what you already know and can do.

Many husbands and wives put their hopes for fulfillment in people or in places, whether homes or vacation spots. To those thirsting for fulfillment, these things look like a quenching pool of water. Yet once they reach them, they find only the sand of a mirage. Only Christ gives everlasting satisfaction.

Probably the most important thing that negative emotions reveal is our own self-centeredness. We need to admit our level of self-centeredness, because out of such an admission comes the freedom to refocus our expectations away from God's creation and onto God Himself.

God has established spiritual laws, or principles, in all relationships, especially marriage. It's our responsibility to discover these principles, measure our lives by them, and correct any behavior that is "off center" from God's best.

The "quest for success" comes with a high price tag. Many women and men spend years of their lives climbing the ladder of success—only to find when they reach the top that the ladder is leaning against the wrong wall. Status and titles do little to light up our lives—they can never take the places of family and God.

ransfer the ownership and authority of your life, including your marriage, to God (see Galatians 2:20). Establish God's Word and the leading of the Holy Spirit as your final authority (see Psalm 19:11). Expect God, through Christ, to meet all your needs (see Philippians 4:19).

e live overflowing lives because the *Source* of life, instead of the *gifts* (people, places, possessions, and position) of life, brings us contentment. How? By leading us to the well that never runs dry.

*H*ave you never counted on the road of life and marriage being as rough as it turned out to be? It happens. But maybe you also never counted on a Friend who loves you as much as God does. For He Himself said, "I will never leave you nor forsake you" (Joshua 1:5, NIV).

*W*hen we rejoice in the Lord always, He keeps us, in many situations, from giving in to such temptations as envy, jealousy, fear, and anger. Rejoicing, even in times of testing, is acknowledging that God is the source of life. And it brings us to the place where our lives can be filled by God Himself.

*T*rust God to meet all your needs. This will allow you to take the focus off your own needs. Then refocus your efforts on meeting your spouse's needs, helping him or her in areas of struggle.

*G*od wants us to be mature, loving people who reflect Jesus Christ's character in every area of life, including marriage. The only way He can make that happen is to allow trials. It's important to note that God doesn't *cause* the trials. They come from many sources, including our own sinful nature and Satan, God's enemy. But God uses them for our ultimate benefit.

We honor God by serving Him. Seeing people (like our mate) renewed, healed, blessed, encouraged, and motivated by our love for them increases our self-worth as servants of God.

Learning what your spouse needs and looking for creative ways to meet those needs unlocks the door of serving. Genuine fulfillment comes through knowing and loving God first, and then through serving others in response to His love.

We dishonor God when we live with an attitude of ungratefulness. We know we're ungrateful when we are: constantly comparing what we have with the possessions or positions (or marriages) of others; continually complaining about the way "life" is treating us; always fearful; trying to manipulate others; and so on.

Ungratefulness can be traced to a failure to find benefits in everything we experience and an unwillingness to trust God to fulfill our deepest needs.

Discover More Fuel for Lasting Relationships
in these best-sellers by Gary Smalley and John Trent, Ph.D.

The Language of Love

The way we communicate verbally helps determine how successful we'll be in our marriages, families, and friendships. Excel in all your relationships by learning *The Language of Love*. Through the use of "emotional word pictures," you'll be able to capture people's attention, make your messages memorable, and unlock intimacy as never before. *Paperback with study guide.*

The Two Sides of Love

Do you and your loved ones sometimes seem poles apart? Do you long for greater affection with those you treasure most? *The Two Sides of Love* will help you balance love's hard, authoritative side with its soft, empathetic side and create deeper, more satisfying relationships! *Paperback with study guide* and *book-on-cassette.*

Available at Christian bookstores everywhere.